Father Said

Father Said

Poems by Hal Sirowitz

ISBN: I-932360-27-I

Published bby Soft Skull Press
7I Bond Street, Brooklyn, NY II237

Distributed by Publishers Group West
I.800.788.3I23 | www.pgw.com

Cataloging-in Publication Data for this title available from the Library of Congress.

The author wishes to thank the Corporation of Yaddo and the Virginia Center for the Creative Arts for awarding him residencies during which he worked on these poems. He also thanks the following magazines and anthologies for supporting his work and publishing some of these poems—*About Poetry.com*; *Bellevue Literary Review*; *Barrow Street*; *Fence*; *Goodfoot*; *Green Mountain Poetry Review*; *Gulfstreaming*; *Homestead Review*; *Manhattan Poetry Review*; *One Hundred + Poets Against the War* (Salt Press); *NthPosition.com*; *One Hundred Writers Speak Out about September 11* (NYU Press); *Ploughshares*, edited by Cornelius Eady; *Poems for Lord Hutton*, edited by Todd Swift; *Saint Ann's Review*; and *Zeek*.

When I was little, we had an argument

about whether we should eat the vegetables or meat or the things we liked or disliked first. So I began

eating my food in alphabetical order. You have to know how to spell, though.

From *And I Thought I Was Crazy*

by Judy Reiser

Contents

What We Can Learn

Flies Love You 2

Ducks at Peace 3

Two Rabbits in a Room 4

The Steak's Previous Life 5

If That Fly Could Talk 6

Squirrel Problem 7

What We Can Learn from Ants 8

How to Be a Humanitarian 9

The Deer on the Side of the Road .10

Saving a Spider's Life 11

Being Nice to the Birds 12

Mosquito Bite 13

Knowing Them Through Their Pets 14

Not to Have Died in Vain 15

Two Ends of a Cat 16

I Wasn't the One Who Killed It 17

Kitty Litter 18

Same Species, Different Sex 19

Saluting the Bull 20

Doggie Bag 21

Racing to Oblivion

When Autumn Leaves Have
Almost Finished Falling 24

Trusting My Feet 25

Bad Drivers 26

The Other Side of the Car 27

Entering a New State 28

The Wrecking Ball 29

Visiting Japan 30
Rearranging the Speedometer 31
Meeting Place 32
Water, Water Everywhere 33
Tit for Tat 34
The Story of a Jerk 35
Blocking My View 36

The Road Back

Snobs 38
The Shrunken Version 39
The Lost Friend 40
The War at Home 41
When I Used to Cook 42
The Substitute for Swings 43
Substituting Husbands 44
Nothing Much to Share 45
Holding On to the Chains 46
How Her Liver Was Saved 47
Buying Him a Bar 48
War Wounds 49
Asking for Her Hand 50
The Loan 51
Sharing the Pain 52

The Male Advantage

What's There to Explore 54
The Long Leash 55
Sight Unseen 56
In the Lion's Mouth 57
The Male Advantage 58
What I'm Known For 59

Imitation Wood 60

Inside/Outside 61

Getting Rid of Her 62

Rotten Personality 63

The Subject Was Always Roses 64

The Cost of Talking 65

Zebra-Striped Sports Jacket 66

The Kingdom Under Siege 67

The Natural 68

Losing My Place 69

The Dead Don't Return What You Leant Them 70

Trouble in Gossip Land 71

Ten Minutes Ahead 72

What House Was He Talking About 73

The Hawk Who Became a Dove 74

The Listener 75

Being a Good Citizen 76

The World Belongs to the Young 77

Divorce Was Never a Possibility

The Absence of Light 80

The Price of Marriage 81

Tell Her I'm Not Here 82

When Words Come Easy 83

Holding On to My Tongue 84

Correcting an Unbalance 85

What Do You Mean When You Say You Love Me 86

The Mistake 87

Mutual Trust 88

The Woman's Fault 89

It Takes Two to Avoid Someone 90

Wondering When to Return 91

Why God Created Eve 92

The Sound of a Tree Falling 93

The Cost of a New Hairdo 94

She Likes Her Twenties Crisp 95

The Extra Pounds Belong to Her 96

Letting the Washing Machine Decide 97

Upgrading the Bungalow 98

Pointing Out Progress 99

How to Be a Gentleman 100

The Hair on My Head 101

The Silent Divorce 102

By the Time He Got to India 103

How to Avoid Being Idle

How to Build Confidence 106

How to Avoid Being Idle 107

Facts About Grammar 108

The Price of Being Alone 109

Similar Brains 110

The Use of Facts 111

Talking During the Commercials 112

The Benefits of Ignorance 113

The Correct Distance from a Crocodile 114

The Benefits of an Active Lifestyle 115

Lengthy Services 116

What Waking Up Means 117

Cutting Down Costs 118

The Pursuit of Laziness 119

What Followed Your Birth 120

Undecided 121

Abandoning the Declaration 122

Doesn't Matter What It Looks Like 123

Saving It for Later 124

No Place for It to Go 125

Tight Bathing Suits 126

The Art of Marriage 127

The Movies She Picks 128

No Signs of Getting Better 129

Misery Loves Company 130

Only Your Eyes Seem to Work 131

The Need to Get Away 132

Getting Me Steamed 133

Worth Bending Down For 134

Practicing for That Day 135

Spring Cleaning Came Early 136

Mother of Invention 137

The Peanut Count 138

Reusing Words 139

The Joke That Got No Laughs 140

Taking Your Fun While You Can 141

As I Lay Dying

To Coincide 144

God's Delivery System 145

Dressing Up for a Possible Memory 146

Taking Longer Than Your Mother 147

Choice of Diseases 148

When the Body Breaks Down 149

Six-Shooter 150

A Call from Death Valley 151

The Trapped Sardine 152

Escape from the Hospital 153

Among Familiar Surroundings 154

Saving a Spot for Me in Heaven 155

One Organ Too Many 156

Four Thumbs Are Better Than Two 157

Why There Are No Miracles 158

Dying Once Is Enough 159

Pushing the Future Further Ahead 160

All the Dead I've Known 161

The News of My Teeth 162

God's Laugh 163

Cemetery Plot & Stone 164

A Crooked Man 165

What to Save for Death 166

Half Dead 167

Daily Lotto 168

Father Said

What We Can Learn

Flies Love You

If you want fewer flies in the house,
Father said, you have to close the door
behind you faster. You never see
any flies following me, because if
they were behind me they'd get squashed
by the door. But when you go outside
they surround you, because they know
you're their ticket to free room & board.
By the time you close the door they
already have their immediate family
inside, plus a few relatives. They
don't have to stay in the house long,
because they could leave with you too.
You make it so easy for them to come
& go I bet they use our house for their
permanent address. Yet, they never
give you thanks. They
bite you while you're sleeping.

Ducks at Peace

I'd like to take my family to the lake,
Father said, so they can see how well
the animal & fish kingdoms get along.
You hardly ever see ducks fighting.
If they do, it's done in private.
We should follow their example,
& not air out our dirty laundry in public.
That was what I told your mother
at the restaurant, that she should
save her complaints for when we
get home. She said she had already
complained there. She was hoping
she'd get better results if she changed locations.

Two Rabbits in a Room

If you put a male & female rabbit
inside a room, Father said, & shut off
the lights, you'll soon get bunnies.
Humans don't work that way. A guy
first has to talk a woman into being alone
with him in a room, then he has to get
permission to turn off the lights.
That's only the beginning. You're
too young for me to explain the other steps.
One day you'll be in a room with someone.
Maybe she'll be the one to shut off the lights.
Don't think that just because a step
got skipped your job is going to be easy. She
may make the next step take forever.
Don't get hung up on the steps. Sometimes
it's easier just to get another woman.

The Steak's Previous Life

You shouldn't judge a steak
by the first bite, Father said.
You're committing a grave injustice
to the cow. Put yourself in that cow's
shoes for a moment—or to be more correct,
its hooves—& imagine how you'd feel
if you ate grass your whole life—
just the color of it makes me sick—
so you'd taste nice & tender. Instead
of being appreciated you're thrown away.
You'd feel like your life was wasted.
Why don't you put the meaning back
into that cow's life & take a second bite.
The next time we pass one on the highway,
on the way to the hotel in the country,
you'll be able to look at it without feeling guilty.

If That Fly Could Talk

If I don't kill that fly, Father said,
then I'm letting it defeat me.
Who is more powerful—that little thing
or a big husky fellow like me?
You'd think it'd try to avoid me,
but it keeps buzzing in my ear,
as if it's hoping to find something there.
I keep sticking my finger in my ear,
then pulling it out to show that fly
nothing is inside. But my ear canal
must remind him of its last home.
If only that fly could talk I know
we could reach an understanding—
if it'll leave my ear alone I'll reward it
by not taking its life. But the only talk
it understands is its death.

Squirrel Problem

Don't feed the squirrels in front of the house,
Father said. They'll think they live here,
& move into the attic. Do it in front
of the neighbor's house. Let them be
his problem. But don't let him catch you
more than once. The second time
he notices you doing it he'll accuse you
of trying to relocate the squirrels from
your house to his. They go where
the food is. That's why when I spot
an acorn near the house I quickly
get rid of it. Leaving it there would
be like giving them their welcome mat.

What We Can Learn from Ants

You shouldn't kill an ant,
Father said, unless you absolutely
have to. They have as much right
to the backyard as you. In fact,
they have more. Their ancestors
were here before ours even got
on the boat. You should learn
to respect life-forms different
from your own. Who can say
we're so much more superior? I've
never seen them being idle. I
wish I could say the same thing about you.

How to Be a Humanitarian

Instead of waiting for the fly to stay still,
Father said, so I could kill it with the fly swatter,
I decided to take a more humane approach.
I opened the window & waited for it to go outside.
Meanwhile, three other flies flew in. I wanted
to be a humanitarian, but they were forcing me
into being a mass killer. Then I had a brilliant idea.
I shut off the lights. The buzzing soon stopped.
They had no difficulty finding the exit in the dark.
That's why I have no pity for those who
commit murder & say they didn't want to do it.
If I could find a way not to kill a fly, they could just
as easily have found a way not to take another person's life.

The Deer on the Side of the Road

There are all these signs on the road
warning you to slow down for deer,
Father said. But did they ever think
of asking the deer to slow down for us?
Of course not. Since they're animals
they're allowed to be irresponsible.
But if I hit one of them I'll damage my car.
Just like the lion is the king of the jungle
the deer is becoming king of the road.
Noah saved them from the Flood
by building an ark. After all these years
you'd think they'd want to return the favor
by staying out of our way when we're driving.

Saving a Spider's Life

Instead of killing the spider, Father said,
as your mother requested, I grabbed
one of its legs & carried the spider outside.
It jumped out of my hand before I
could put it on the ground, leaving
a leg behind. Since it still had seven left
I didn't feel as bad. I achieved what
your mother had wanted without shedding
blood, or whatever their insides contain.
Plus, I got out of doing chores in the kitchen.
She wouldn't let me go near her
no matter how many times I washed my hands.

Being Nice to the Birds

I'll let you have these breadsticks,
Father said, if you promise
to use them to feed the birds.
They're not to be used for target practice.
It confuses a bird to get hit on the head
by the exact same thing it's eating.
The bird doesn't know whether
to continue eating or to fly away.
How would you like it if while eating
your mother's meatloaf I threw
a big piece of mine at you? It
might scar you for life.
Why do that to a bird? Let them eat in peace.

Mosquito Bite

Just because a mosquito bit your mother,
Father said, doesn't give her the right
to take it out on me. She should have
gotten the mosquito back. It's another
example of how the people closest
to the scene of the crime are the ones
who suffer the most. I wish it had
bitten me instead. Eventually
the swelling will go away, but
to get your mother to stop
bothering me takes a lot longer.

Knowing Them Through Their Pets

You can find out a lot about a woman
by watching how she treats her pet,
Father said. And if she doesn't have one,
that tells a lot about her too. What
that says I'm not too sure. You might
try taking her to the park where you
could watch her interact with someone
else's dog. It's not the same as watching
her play with her own. But you have to
substitute what you can't do with what you can.
It's like going on a trip and forgetting
to bring a toothbrush. There's nothing
else you could do but use your finger.

Not to Have Died in Vain

At the picnic the ant made a big mistake,
Father said. It thought your mother's arm
was a hill. The ant's death would not have
been in vain if you could learn from its mistake.
It should have gotten another ant to go up
the hill first to make sure it was safe.

The Two Ends of a Cat

Your sister says she loves the cat,
Father said, but it's your mother
who cleans her bowl & changes
her kitty litter. She does the dirty work.
Your sister does the enjoyable jobs—she
feeds & brushes her. She only deals with
the front of the cat & leaves the back half
for your mother. But a cat has both a front
& a back. By right she should be taking turns & not
leave your mother in charge of the most difficult part.

I Wasn't the One Who Killed It

Your mother & sister were upset
that I had driven over a dead cat,
Father said, but I figured since it
was already dead one more car
crushing it wouldn't make
that much difference. Of course,
I felt sorry for the cat, but not enough
to stop the car, move the dead cat from the road,
& bury it. There was always the risk
of my getting hit by another driver
while I was bending down to pick it up.
I didn't want my death to overshadow the cat's.

Kitty Litter

Your sister hardly ever changes the kitty litter,
Father said, so your mother thought of a way
to get her to do it more often. She moved it
from the bathroom to your sister's room.
The only problem was that by being
in that location the smell drifted to the other rooms
& stunk up the house so she had to put it back.
Now if she wants
to make a point,
she has to take your sister
to where it is,
rather than bringing it to her.

Same Species, Different Sex

If you put a cat & dog in the same room,
Father said, they're not going to get along.
They're different species. But your sister
& you are very much alike—you have
the same parents. So how come when you're
together you fight like cats & dogs? The
only major difference is sex, but you should
be able to overcome that. If not, how are you
ever going to get married? Brothers who couldn't
get along with their sisters usually end up
as bachelors & I'm sure you don't want that.

Saluting the Bull

Your mother & I went to a bullfight,
Father said, while we were in Spain. We
saw a matador get stabbed by the horns
of a bull. The matador was taken away
before he could lose more blood.
Your mother felt sorry for the matador.
She was worried that his costume was ruined.
I felt sorry for the bull. How would
you like it if someone waved
your least favorite color in your face,
trying to make you look silly
in front of a crowd? The bull never
asked to be put in that ring. But only
the matador got what he deserved—
a wound. The bull didn't deserve
what he got—an early death.

Doggie Bag

You're not required to have a dog
in order to ask for a doggie bag,
Father said. Walking out of
a restaurant with one of those bags
shows the other customers that you
possess self-control. It doesn't matter
how much is in the bag because no one
can see what's inside. What counts is
that you have a bag. Even if you end up
throwing it away it wasn't a total waste.
For a few days it served as a souvenir.

Racing to Oblivion

When Autumn Leaves Have Almost Finished Falling

Your mother tells me to drive slower,
Father said, so she can look at the leaves.
I don't recall her ever looking at them before.
But she said that this was the last weekend
to see them. I find it hard to get excited
about a bunch of dying leaves. It's probably
because I'm the one who has to rake the backyard.
If she had to do it she'd wish they'd stay
on the branches permanently. So I continue
driving at the same speed, but whenever I
have to stop at a traffic light I point out
as many dying leaves as I can to make up for the ones she missed.

Trusting My Feet

I measured the exact distance I was
parked from the fire hydrant, Father said,
so I was shocked when I saw the ticket.
I decided to argue my case in court.
The judge asked to see my tape measure.
I said I used what I had—my two feet.
He said that wasn't scientific enough.
I said they haven't changed in twenty years,
which makes them very reliable. If a man
can't trust his feet, then what can he trust?
Not only did I have to pay the fine, but
I lost out on some business, because I
had to take off to show up for court.
I still believe in my innocence. The cop
probably didn't have a tape measure either.
The only reason I got a ticket was
his feet must have been bigger than mine.

Bad Drivers

Your mother doesn't like me honking
at bad drivers, Father said, but that's
the reason cars have horns. She's afraid
one of those drivers is going to shoot me.
But if they don't know how to drive properly,
I seriously doubt they'd know how to shoot.
Why should I allow an incompetent person
to keep making turns without looking? He's
going to endanger others. The driver he'll hit
may not have my reflexes. They'll get into
a big crash, & a few might die. But if I embarrass
him by making everyone stare at him he just
might change & start looking both ways before
making a turn. The world would be a safer place,
because I wasn't afraid to use my horn.

The Other Side of the Car

Once I banged into another car,
Father said. Since mine was bigger
I knew I'd have less damage. He
wanted to exchange phone numbers
of insurance companies, but I
told him we'd be doing ourselves
a favor by not reporting it. We don't
want our rates to go up. He agreed.
When he drove away I had to laugh
at how gullible he was. But when
I arrived home & took a closer look
at my car I stopped laughing.
I had more damage than I had thought.
I was so busy trying to talk him into doing what
I wanted I forgot to look at both sides of my car.

Entering a New State

The map could be correct, Father said.

The boulevard's name might have been changed.

Or maybe we're already in the next state.

I don't ever remember leaving New York.

That's why we should always be on the look-out

for signs saying, "You are now entering a new state."

It's important to say goodbye so we know where we are.

The Wrecking Ball

When we were in Italy, Father said,
your mother took me to see the Leaning Tower
of Pisa. I couldn't see why people make
such a big commotion over it. Where
I work I see the real thing—buildings
getting torn down all the time. Why should
I be impressed with one that hasn't fallen yet?

Visiting Japan

Though the temples in Japan
were truly magnificent, Father said,
they didn't offset the discomfort
I felt at having to eat so close to the floor.
The Japanese prefer to squat than sit.
When I sit I have the support of the chair
to hold me up. But when I squat I have
to support myself with my hands, or I
lean too much to one side. My elbow
kept going into your mother's miso soup.
She said it tasted better without my elbow in it.
It's easy for the Japanese to squat because they
use chopsticks, which require only one hand.
But for people like me, who need to use two hands—
one for the fork, the other for the knife—it's much too difficult.

Rearranging the Speedometer

When your mother complains about
my driving I can't tell her to take a bus,
Father said. I say, "I'm going slower,"
& hope she doesn't lean over to read
the speedometer. Once, with the help
of a screwdriver, I fixed it so the needle
would stay on the number fifteen
no matter how fast I was driving.
The only problem was I didn't know
how fast I was driving either. I had
to take it to a mechanic to get it fixed.

Meeting Place

If we happen to get lost,
Father said, go to the car
& wait for me. I wish
I could leave the door open,
so you could wait inside,
but if I did there's a good chance
the car might not be there.
I'm sorry if getting lost costs you
some discomfort—standing out there
in the cold—but if I make it too easy
you're liable to do it all the time.
If you find that your mind is drifting
& you're not paying attention to my movements,
try to snap out of it. Or at least wait
until the end of the day when there are
less people around & you'll be easier to find.

Water, Water Everywhere

During the downpour the roads were flooded,
Father said. Your mother wanted me to wait
until the water got lower, but that might have taken hours.
I drove through it. When the water started to seep
through the bottom I didn't think it was prudent
to stop & try to find the leak. I didn't have
anything to plug it up with. She kept
saying we might drown. The water wasn't
deep enough, so I kept going forward
while she went backwards in her mind,
recalling a flood she had witnessed as a young girl.
I wasn't interested about one from her past.
I only cared about the one we were in now.
After making it through without the motor stalling
I made a joke, saying if I had known it was this deep
I'd have brought along a fishing rod to stick out
the window. Just because her shoes were wet
wasn't a good enough reason not to find it funny.

Tit for Tat

I once parked my car the exact distance
the law requires from a fire hydrant,
Father said. I was shocked to find
a ticket on my window. I realized
the driver of the car behind me had
pushed me half a foot closer
to the hydrant to get into his space.
Six inches was all I needed to prevent
myself from getting a ticket. I made
sure upon leaving the spot to also give
his car a shove—not that it did me any good—
but at least the one I gave will last longer.
Once I paid my fine I forgot all about it,
but he had to get the scratches fixed to forget his.

The Story of a Jerk

This guy steals my parking space
right in front of my nose, Father said.
He saw me waiting for it. He figured
that since I had my wife with me I
couldn't make a scene. He figured
wrong. I did make one, but she stopped
me from making it bigger. I called him
almost every dirty word I could think of,
except for those pertaining to the female anatomy.
After she made me drive away she said I had
to learn to be more careful, that his brother-in-law
could have been a gangster. She's always
making strangers more powerful than they are.
If he does have a family they couldn't be on good terms,
because he's a full-time jerk. I could tell it wasn't
a pose. He was too good at it to be acting.

Blocking My View

They say on a clear day
 you can see forever but that's
hard to do when your mother
is blocking my view, Father said.
When I kindly asked her to move
to the side she said, "Why look
at a mountain when you can look at me?"
I keep wishing she was more like
a mountain, that she'd stay in one spot
and not be able to watch my every move.

36

The Road Back

Snobs

You can tell we come from a distinguished family
by the fact that most of our relatives want to have
nothing to do with us, Father said.
One cousin studied to become a dentist,
but he never put all those years of schooling
to use. He married money. He
never had to work. What he does
with his time I have no way of knowing,
but I can't imagine it being much fun.
Now that I've moved to his town
I should let him know we're neighbors.
But I wouldn't want to make him unhappy.
He lives in a mansion with an armed guard.
I live in a small apartment. But no one would
know that just by looking at our zip codes.

The Shrunken Version

The older you get the less you look
like me, Father said, & the more you
start to look like my father. I get
confused sometimes & almost call you
by his name. Then I wonder what
could have made him shrink. When
I take a closer look I realize you don't
resemble him as much as I had thought.
I feel relieved, because if the resemblance
was too strong I'd worry that you might
have also inherited his tendency of giving away
his money to everyone but me.

The Lost Friend

When I was young I once played
hide & seek with a friend,
Father said. He hid so well
that I never saw him again.
I always expected that one day
we'd bump into each other
and the game would finally end.
He should have chosen a nicer way
of saying goodbye. I wondered
what I did that was so horrible.
The only thing I could think of
was I once cheated him out of a quarter.
But if I stole money from you
wouldn't you have tried to see me
one last time to ask for it back?

The War at Home

Your great-grandfather was born in America,
Father said, which makes you fourth generation.
So don't worry if your friends keep asking why
I didn't fight in the Second World War.
Just because I didn't serve abroad
doesn't make me less of an American.
You can't be less of what you already are.
I had to stay home to take care of my sick parents.
I did my share of fighting. "Dad, it's not cheaper
not taking your medicine," I had to keep saying.
"If you get sicker it'd cost even more." "Mom,
I can't just marry a rich woman. Making money
that way will make me lose my self-respect."
It was a struggle. They fought me tooth & nail.
I'd rather have fought a real enemy.
It's always harder fighting your own kind.

When I Used to Cook

My sister eloped & left me
to take care of two sick parents,
Father said. I knew nothing about
cooking. I just stuck the meat
in the oven & prayed it didn't
get too burnt. Now that my parents
are dead I don't cook anymore.
I only remember the praying part,
because I still do it. I pray
that your mother doesn't burn
our dinner again & if she does,
she won't be too insulted if I don't eat it.

The Substitute for Swings

When I was a child,
I liked going to the playground too,
Father said. Then one day I realized
I was getting bored of the swings.
As soon as I got on I wanted to get off.
Luckily that happened just when I was
starting to notice girls. I made the transition
to having crushes on girls without feeling
I was losing much. Girls were a different type
of fun. The major difference was you never
felt like you could get tired of them.
Though, they often got tired of you.

Substituting Husbands

Your aunt's first husband didn't
want her to leave him, Father said.
At one point we were afraid he was
going to kill her. He followed her
to prevent her from going out
with other men. I thought it was
too early for her to start dating.
She had to give the marriage time
to die. She was trying to do it
too quickly. Eventually, he left
her alone. Though when she
married again her next husband
was only different on the outside—
plump where the other one was thin—
but inside, where it counted, he was
very similar. He expected her
to support him. I told her it should
be the other way around, but that was
how she preferred her men.

Nothing Much to Share

I knew too much about your aunt's husband's
other life—the one he spent at bars—
to have liked him, Father said. But I still
treated him with respect. We got along,
even though we didn't have much in common.
He liked to drink. I didn't. He was
always inviting me to stop by at his bar
on my way home from work.
But what would I have done there—
watch him drink? I had already seen him do that.

Holding On to the Chains

When I was a kid I'd swing so high,
Father said, that the adults in the playground
were worried about my safety. I told them
not to worry, that I wouldn't let go
of the swings. Then one day I fell.
That was the end of my adventures
in the sky. From then on if I thought
I was in any danger, I made sure
to do it while I was on the ground.

How Her Liver Was Saved

Your aunt's husband loved to buy others drinks,
Father said. He wasn't satisfied just getting himself
drunk. Everyone at the bar had to be drunk too.
He even got your aunt drinking. I told her
it was bad for her liver. She said if she stopped
drinking with him she'd never see him. I said
it's easier to get a new husband than it is
to replace a liver. But luckily, he stopped
drinking with her. He claimed she made him
talk too much, which lessened the amount he could drink.
He never had any trouble finding livers to ruin.

Buying Him a Bar

Your aunt & her husband are seldom together,
Father said. Whenever I stopped by to visit,
he was working at the bar, drinking up all his profits.
In the old days the police used to call her & she
had to come get him. He was always getting lost.
He couldn't find his way home. She decided
to buy him a bar, so he wouldn't have any need
to leave the neighborhood. She claimed
this marriage was a lot better than her first one.
Since they hardly saw each other they had little to argue about.

War Wounds

Each time we visit your uncle
he finds some excuse
to show us his war wounds, Father said.
I can't tell you how many times
I had to watch him roll up his pants' leg.
But it always looks the same, miniscule.
He keeps promising to show us the one
on his ass, but since there was always
a woman in the room he hasn't been able to.
I don't have to see it to know he was
facing the wrong way. If he fought
those Germans as bravely as he claimed
shouldn't that injury be in the front?
What probably happened was when
he heard explosions for the first time
he got so scared that he rolled into a ball
& left his rear end unprotected. So why
should I feel sorry for him if it hurts
whenever he sits down? Mine hurts too
from having to sit for hours listening to the same old stories.

Asking for Her Hand

When I asked your mother to marry me,
Father said, she didn't give me an answer
right away. She said she needed time
to think about it. The next day she said yes,
but apparently she hasn't stopped thinking
about it. Whenever she's mad I have to hear
about all the others who asked—
the rabbi, the doctor, & a couple of other
lofty professions. But what she never mentions
is whether any of them had asked
a second time. I'd have kept asking
until she had gotten tired of saying no.

The Loan

Your mother & I had to pay
for our own wedding, Father said,
so we couldn't invite too many.
We invited both our parents,
though neither of them came.
At first it was embarrassing
not to have them there, but
then I got to thinking, They
gave us life & for that we
should be grateful. So I never
held any grudge against her father.
I accepted his limitations. He
never gave us a wedding present,
but a few years later when I needed
money he let me borrow some.
I paid him back with interest.
I gave him a better rate than the bank.
Yet, whenever he visits he's always bringing it up—
"Remember when I lent you money?" I stop myself
from saying, "I also remember you making a profitt."

Sharing the Pain

I went to hear the writer Ben Hecht speak
at a Madison Square Garden rally,
Father said. He gave us firsthand stories
about how the Nazis were exterminating
the Jews by forcing them
into gas ovens. We all knew what was
going on, but we were afraid to speak out.
We didn't want people to think this was
a Jewish war. They'd want our government
to pull out. We had to share the pain
of the war, even though it wasn't evenly distributed.
We could never get the credit for being
the main victims. Whenever a little old Italian
or Irish lady knocked on my door asking for donations
to help the parents of those who lost their sons,
I gladly gave more than I could afford,
even though I knew every Italian or Irish guy
who died had a fifty/fifty chance of surviving.
He could always shoot first. But the Jews
who were cremated in the ovens—all they had
to defend themselves with were their prayers.

The Male Advantage

What's There to Explore

If I wasn't married, Father said,
I'd have been an explorer. Since
the only truly unexplored places
are the moon & beyond & I
don't want to go there, I'd have
to go to partially explored places,
& hope there was still something left
I could give my name to, like a mountain.
Then there'd be a Sirowitz Mountain.
I'd have to hope that future settlers wouldn't change it.
But I got married & had a family, so all that
is just a fantasy. Instead, I explore the reasons
you're having trouble in school. Was it because you
had not studied enough? Or did you get nervous
during the test & forget everything? I hope we find out soon,
so we can explore a more interesting subject.

The Long Leash

You see the leash on that dog? Father said.
It's so long that he doesn't even know
it's connected to him. That's what I do
with your mother. I give her a long leash.
She thinks she's the boss. But why do I
have to let her think she's in control?
Isn't the one paying the bills legally in charge?
If that's the case then this household is
being run illegally. But try getting the police
to uphold the law. They're trained to look
the other way when there's a domestic dispute.
I could never dream of getting a divorce.
She gives me a tough time as it is.
Imagine what she'd be like if she hated me.

Sight Unseen

I'm probably the only man who bought a house
without his wife ever seeing it, Father said.
In fact, I didn't even see it. That took
a lot of courage. It also took a lot of imagination,
because when she asked me to tell her what the house
looked like I had to make it up. I tried
to describe it in general terms—the bedroom
was here, the living room was there. I figured
they had to be near each other, so I couldn't
be wrong. When she moved in she wanted to know
if it was the right house, because it was
very different from how I described it. I
told her I saw a few houses that day & must
have gotten confused. The main drawback
was the width of the hallway. It was
too narrow for two people. One had to come
to a full stop to let the other squeeze through.
I kept telling your sister that the halls
were only to be used for traveling between rooms.
I had to step over her a few times.

In the Lion's Mouth

Remember the lion tamer at the circus,
Father said, & how he put his head
in the lion's mouth. I was impressed
until I realize the lion had no teeth.
I do the equivalent with your mother,
but it's a lot more dangerous.
Except for two molars, she
has all her original teeth. Each time
she asks me how I like her cooking
my head is in the same spot as the lion tamer's.
That my head is still intact after all these years
of marriage is proof of how quickly I respond.

The Male Advantage

What gives us an edge over women,
Father said, is we get out of the bathroom faster.
The few extra seconds give us
a large advantage. While they're
still sitting on the toilet we're
already zipping up our flies. We
get to our next appointments quicker.
The more women use the bathroom
the more those seconds add up.
Seconds turn into minutes. Minutes
turn into hours. I hope you remember this
whenever you're in the bathroom. The longer
you spend tucking in your shirt the more
you're in danger of becoming like them.

What I'm Known For

I spent a lot of money buying
expensive suits to impress people,
Father said. Yet no one remembers
what suit I wore the day before.
They only remember the day I went
to work wearing my pajama top.
I woke up late & was in a rush. I
forgot to put on my white shirt.
You never know what people will
remember you for. If I had known
it'd be for coming to work wearing
pajamas I'd have spent more money
on them than on those suits.

Imitation Wood

They say you should knock
on wood for good luck,
Father said, but nowadays
most tables look like they're
made from wood but aren't.
So I suggest we knock on
each other's arms. We'll use
our flesh in place of wood.
What counts is knocking
on something that's authentic.

Inside/Outside

My engagement to your mother
was as enjoyable, Father said,
as sticking a finger in a cake
and licking off the icing.
Marriage is like cutting the cake
and discovering the inside
has nothing to do with the outside.

Getting Rid of Her

You won't have to worry about where
you're going to be buried, Father said,
because I got you a cemetery plot. It's
too bad I can't find you a girlfriend,
because it seems like you need me
to take care of that too. You haven't
done well in that department. I hope
you get rid of the one you have.
She didn't know what to say when
I asked her if she liked taking care
of you. It seemed like she was
waiting for you to marry her before
she'd even start. She should
at least have given you a preview—
cook you dinner instead of making you
take her out to restaurants every night—
& not leave it to your imagination.

Rotten Personality

The woman your sister wanted
to introduce you to is already
a vast improvement over your
last girlfriend, Father said.
She at least smiles. That one
made me wonder if she had teeth.
When she finally smiled—only
because she knew the evening
would soon be over—I realized
her lack of charm had nothing
to do with her teeth. She just had
a rotten personality. She didn't
like the restaurant, because she claimed
the restroom was too small.
I sent your mother in to take a look.
She said it was large enough for her,
& your mother is a larger woman.
If she was critical about the restroom
I knew it wouldn't be long before
she'd be critical of you.

The Subject Was Always Roses

Whenever I complained about something
to your uncle, Father said, he'd say,
"Stop and smell the roses." Finally,
I couldn't take it anymore & I said,
"Where are those roses you keep wanting
me to smell? I don't see any." "It's
just an expression," he said. "I'd appreciate
if you don't use the word *roses* again,"
I said, "unless you have some." I knew he
wasn't about to get any. They're past his price range.

The Cost of Talking

They say talk is cheap,
Father said, but it costs
me money whenever
your mother does it.
She talks herself into
thinking we need
a new blender. Once
we get it she misses
the old one. I keep
telling her the less
we buy the less she'll miss.

Zebra-Striped Sports Jacket

The stripes on a zebra help it
to blend into the jungle, Father said,
so its enemies won't be able to see it.
But those same stripes on me
make me stand out. That's why
I got this zebra-striped sports jacket.
I won't always have to stay close
to your mother, because she wouldn't
be afraid of losing me. She wouldn't
fail to find me in a crowd. In fact,
she'd be able to spot me a hundred
yards away. I'd be free to roam around.
She couldn't accuse me of deserting her,
because she'd always be able to find me.

The Kingdom Under Siege

A father is like a king, Father said.
His every word should be obeyed.
But when the queen berates him
in front of his subjects, his kingdom
ends up in shambles. By constantly
undermining my authority, your mother
has planted the seeds of her own destruction.
Your sister must have gotten the idea
of insubordination from your mother.
I try to stay out of their battles unless I've been
asked to help. Your sister isn't appreciative
of my help. "Fuck you," she says. It's
like the French Revolution is happening again,
but instead of people getting their heads
chopped off we find a solution. We send her
to her friend's house to sleep over.

The Natural

Since your mother & I can't agree
on what our problem is—I think
it's her, she thinks it's me—I hope
you haven't minded when at times
we have made it seem like you were
the problem. It couldn't have been
pleasant being a scapegoat, but
so far you've been a natural at it.
We only have to give you one angry look,
& your whole demeanor seems to cry out,
"Why me?" That gets your mother & I
mad for real. Why shouldn't it be you?
Would you rather have your parents
continue to yell at each other? Or would
you like to give them a break by letting them
yell at you instead? You get free room & board.
It's time you did something to earn your keep.
You should be happy your parents are
yelling at you & not at each other.

Losing My Place

Your mother takes me to a foreign movie,
Father said. If I had known I was
going to have to read the whole time,
I'd have stayed home instead & read
my newspaper. The print is easier
on my eyes. But when the actress
did a long scene in her nightgown,
I was so busy watching her that I lost
my place. By the time she got dressed
it was too late to figure out the plot.
It didn't make sense to continue reading.
I couldn't ask your mother what the movie
was about, because she'd know I was
looking at the actress too much.
Women don't like their husbands looking
at other women, especially when they're
wearing nightgowns. So could you do me
a favor & ask her to tell you about the movie?
She'll probably leave out what the woman looked
like in her nightgown, but I already know about that.

The Dead Don't Return What You Lent Them

Your mother just informed me that the neighbor
down the block has died, Father said. I wished
she hadn't lent him my new pair of lawn clippers,
but she felt bad watching him trying to trim the bushes
while his condition kept getting worse & thought
they'd help make his job easier. Now it's
going to be hard to get them back. His wife
may have already promised a neighbor
he could have them. Whatever is mine also belongs
to your mother. We share everything equally
until she lends it out. Then she no longer considers
it ours. It just becomes mine. For it
to become ours again I'd have to get it back.

Trouble in Gossip Land

Your friend's mother prides herself
on being the neighborhood dispenser
of gossip, Father said, but this week
her reputation has taken a big blow.
One neighbor died of cancer. A couple
got divorced. She didn't know about
either, though that's not what
she's telling everyone. I predict
that's she's going to want to create
her very own incident, so she'll be
the first to know about it. She'd
love it if I were in the center of it,
because of my stature on the block—
I have the most expensive car. That's why
I'm on the look-out—if I see her
coming I'll make myself disappear.
If she knocks on our door & asks for me,
tell her I'm not at home. If she's not able
to get to me she'll have to use someone else.

Ten Minutes Ahead

Once I set the clocks ten minutes ahead,
Father said, to help get your mother out
of the house. But she found out what I did
because I forgot to change the car clock. The
entire week I had to put up with her saying,
"You still owe me ten minutes. Use some
of that time to make me tea." I'd say, "I
already gave you back your ten minutes."
"Did you?" she'd say. "It must not have made
much of an impression on me if I forgot."

What House Was He Talking About

If you make a speech it'd help
if you knew what you were talking about,
Father said. It makes the listener
feel more secure. So when you
tell me how much you help
clean the house I can't help thinking,
"Does he mean this house? Or did he
have another one in mind?" Because
I don't remember seeing you working much.
I can't honestly say you dusted the furniture.
I only saw you move the dust around.
They say practice makes perfect. But
in your case I don't need perfection.
Just the fact that you practiced would make me happy.

The Hawk Who Became a Dove

Most people start off supporting
their country's war efforts,
Father said, but as soon as someone
close to them gets drafted,
they suddenly change their tune
& begin to question the government.
Your friend's father was a hawk.
When his son received a draft notice
he became a dove. Instead of swooping down
on anyone opposed to the war, he
started to do lots of cooing. He's
easier to listen to now, because he
isn't always ruffling someone's feathers.
It's a shame that he needed the possibility
of his son's death to improve his personality.

The Listener

One reason your mother & I had you,
Father said, was because we could sense
that your sister wasn't going to be
very appreciative of anything we did for her.
She cried after she had gotten milk.
We wanted a more appreciative baby.
We thought we got that when you were born.
You didn't cry as much. But now you
don't want much to do with us. You want
to go out every night. We feel better
when we know you're in the house, because
if your mother & I stop listening to each other,
at least we have you for an audience.

Being a Good Citizen

I'd hate to have to be homeless,
Father said. It'd be like living
in a fishbowl. I couldn't pick
my nose without someone noticing.
If that person had enough sense
to give me a tissue it wouldn't
be as embarrassing. But most likely
he'd just look at me like I was disgusting
& walk away. That's why I always
give a quarter. I doubt they're going
to use it to buy tissues. But I'm fulfilling
my obligation as a citizen. I'm giving them
the opportunity to better themselves. Citizenship
doesn't require me to stay around to make sure they did.

The World Belongs to the Young

If I had a choice to come back as a ghost,
Father said, I'd turn it down. You're easy
to forget after you're dead. I'd be afraid
no one would know me. It wouldn't
be my world anymore. The world
always belonged to the young. It
didn't belong to me then, because
I was too stupid to take advantage
of my youth. That's why I'm always
begging you to take advantage of yours.

Divorce Was Never a Possibility

The Absence of Light

God works in mysterious ways, Father said.
But he's not half as mysterious as your mother.
He said, Let there be light. And there was light.
I don't see anything mysterious about that.
He did what He said He'd do.
Your mother says, Let's not be late for the movie.
Yet she takes so long getting dressed
that it doesn't pay to go. Then she
gets mad that I don't take her any place.
God created light where there was only darkness.
She only creates confusion.

The Price of Marriage

I'm good at making money, Father said.
Your mother is good at spending it.
You'd think we'd be the perfect match,
but what she spends it on doesn't make
my life better. She claims the improvements
she made in the house benefit me.
But when I sit on the new couch I wonder
if we needed such an expensive one.
The comfort I got sitting on it disappeared
the moment I saw the bill. Nothing is free.
Marrying her cost me my freedom.

Tell Her I'm Not Here

They say absence makes the heart
grow fonder, Father said, so I'm
planning on staying away from the house more
to see if it's true. I'm a little afraid
your mother wouldn't even notice
I was gone. So from time
to time I need you to say to her,
"Do you know where Dad is?
I need to talk to him." Otherwise,
staying away might be wasted on her.
If that's the case then I shouldn't
be hanging out in the cold. I might
as well be staying home watching TV.

When Words Come Easy

Living with your mother is tough,
Father said, but living without her
would be tougher. We've grown
used to each other. After you live
with someone for a long time
you don't have to think about
what to say. The words come
by themselves. I couldn't imagine
living with someone else. I'd hate
to have to think before I spoke.

Holding On to My Tongue

I have to be more careful what I say
about marriage, Father said,
because your mother may think
I'm talking about ours. I can't
make a general statement without her
taking it personally. It'd seem like
I was better off saying nothing, but
even that gets me in trouble.
She'd want to know why I was being so quiet.
"Has the cat got your tongue?" she'd say,
when she knows she's the one who has it.

Correcting an Unbalance

I never listen to commercials, Father said.
They're aimed at trying to sell me something
I don't need. If I do need it I want to know
that the need originated from me & not
from others. I don't want to end up with lots
of junk I'm only going to throw out. Half
the things in this house aren't used. We
only really need food, clothing, shelter,
& of course, each other. You do need me.
Don't you? Your mother never gives me
much opportunity to talk. I'm supposed to listen.
I'm able to talk to you, but it'd please me
if you said something once in a while.

What Do You Mean When You Say You Love Me

When I tell your mother I love her
it may mean I'm trying to avert
a fight, Father said. So when
you tell me you love me
try being more specific. Are
you saying it to get more of
my money? Or is it because you
truly feel it? Otherwise, I worry
that you might be pulling a fast one
like I do with your mother—you're
saying it to stay out of trouble.

The Mistake

I thought I might be making a mistake
marrying your mother, Father said,
but it seemed just as big a mistake not to.
If I was going to make one anyway
I figured it was better to make the one
that left me less lonely. I used our
engagement as a test to see if she'd
remain loyal. I took another friend
along on our dates, so he could help
pay for it. She never objected.
She let me do whatever I wanted.
When we got married all that stopped.
Now I was the one being tested.

Mutual Trust

If your mother & I seem like we never
agree with each other that doesn't mean
we're not getting along, Father said.
Our disagreements are based on mutual trust.
I trust her enough that when she says
I'm wrong she's not saying that because
she thinks I'm wrong. She just can't
let me be right all the time.

The Woman's Fault

Your mother thinks that men
are the cause of all evil,
Father said. But it was
a woman who brought
the knowledge of good
& evil into the world
by biting into an apple.
All Adam did was take
a bite, so Eve wouldn't
feel so lonely. And what
thanks do you think he got
for doing such a good deed?
He got the larger share of the blame.

It Takes Two to Avoid Someone

It takes two to tango,
Father said, but only
one person to clean
the house. Whenever
I try to help your mother
I just get in her way. If
I know where she is
it'll be easier to avoid her.
You can help by being my spy.
I need you to whisper in my ear,
"Mother is now at this location,"
so I'll know not to go there.

Wondering When to Return

Could you find out if it's safe
for me to go back to the house?
Father said. If she's smiling
that means I can come back.
If she acts agitated then I need to stay away
a little longer. I know I shouldn't be
asking you for your mother's emotional
weather report. But there are only so many storms
I can take. But I got one good thing out of the last one.
I don't have to feel guilty anymore about
all the cigarettes I smoked while she was
in the room. Each day the newspapers
have another report about the damage done
by second-hand smoke. But by the way
she was still able to shout I could tell
all the smoke she inhaled didn't affect her lungs.

Why God Created Eve

In the Bible God created
a companion for Adam—
Eve—to keep Adam from being
lonely, Father said. If it was
such a great idea how come
He didn't create one for himself?
That was what went through my mind
when your mother was yelling at me
for not putting the pickles back
in the refrigerator. But they were
already sour. Letting them stay
at room temperature couldn't
have made them taste worse. Later,
when she served the cake & there
wasn't enough for everyone & she
didn't give herself any I was ready
to forgive her until she started
to eat mine. It made me think
God may have created Eve
for the same reason the TV
needed to be invented—He
wanted to make sure He always
had something entertaining to watch.

The Sound of a Tree Falling

Your mother complains about my snoring,
Father said, but she forgets to mention
the times I was awakened in the middle
of the night by the sound celery makes
when you bite into it. At first I thought it was a tree falling
on the house. I almost jumped out of bed,
but when I saw her munching on celery
I knew I was safe. Crackers are just as loud.
They sound like a chainsaw cutting wood.
My snoring is a form of self-defense—
it drowns out the other noises.

The Cost of a New Hairdo

I make sure to tell your mother how beautiful
she looks, how nothing she can do
will enhance her natural beauty,
Father said, so the way she looks won't
cost me money. You might like looking
at a woman's fancy hairdo, but if you
marry her you'll end up paying every time
she goes to the hairdresser. Once
you pay for it you won't like it as much
& will want her to get it done cheaper.
But a fancy hairdo only comes in one price range—
expensive. The hours you'll have
to work to pay for her hairdresser
will make you get home so late
her hair will already be in curlers
& you won't be able to see what it looked like.

She Likes Her Twenties Crisp

Your mother has gotten so good
at acting like she's in charge,
Father said, there are some days
even I believe her. But when
she asks me for spending money
there's no doubt about who's the boss.
Sometimes she'll get cocky & complain
that one of the twenties I gave her
was too wrinkled. I tell her they're worth
the same no matter how they look. But
she prefers a new one. It's just a ploy
to get me to open my wallet again.
After I give her a new one she suddenly
decides I was right—& asks if she can keep
both of them. Once in a while I'll
let her get away with it. It's the same
as giving to a private charity. I'm making
a donation to get her to leave me alone.

The Extra Pounds Belong to Her

Just because your mother is on a diet,
Father said, doesn't mean I have to be
on one too. How is my loss of a few pounds
going to help her? The only way
she can get skinnier is to lose those pounds herself.
But she insists on serving me this new concoction—
a hamburger without much fat. It doesn't
taste anything like the original. In fact, if
it had no taste, that'd be an improvement.

Letting the Washing Machine Decide

When your mother tells me don't I think
it's time we got a better washing machine,
Father said, I tell her, Let it decide.
If it breaks down, we'll get a better one.
So far it has been taking my side. But
I don't expect to be lucky forever.
Hopefully we'll move before I have to replace it.
Then it'll be the next owner's problem.

Upgrading the Bungalow

Last summer your mother wanted to go away,
Father said. I thought I could rest better
by staying home. But our house wasn't good
enough for her. She wanted some far off place.
I had to rent a bungalow. She complained
the bathroom was too small. I told her
the one at home was larger. We should
have stayed there. She said if I said that
one more time she'd scream & embarrass me.
But we were in the middle of nowhere,
so I told her to go ahead & scream.
She said she was saving her lungs
for later when there were some people around.
We moved to a bungalow with a bigger bathroom.

Pointing Out Progress

Just because you've changed
your underwear doesn't mean
you've made progress, Father said.
For progress to have occurred
the change has to be significant.
If you have to keep pointing out
to people how you've changed—
like, "Look at the way I'm wearing
my shirt. I now tuck in the bottom."—
they're going to say to one another, "Who cares?
He should have been doing that ages ago."

How to Be a Gentleman

You don't have to know what a gentleman is
to be able to act like one, Father said. All you have
to do is keep doing the opposite
of what you've been doing & it
won't take you long to become one.

The Hair on My Head

Your mother accuses me of doing
as many things wrong as I have
hairs on my head, Father said. Even
though I had shown her that my hair
was getting thinner & doesn't
grow as abundantly as it did before,
she continues to use the same analogy.
You'd think she'd at least try to make
her remarks more relevant, but she
keeps repeating the same old phrases.
It proves that being overly critical isn't easy.
I shouldn't be complaining that she's becoming lackadaisical.

The Silent Divorce

Everyone thought the couple at the end
of the block was happy, Father said,
until we found out they were getting divorced.
No one knows what goes on behind closed doors.
You'd think we'd have heard yelling, or noticed
other signs. But their marriage was
so quiet even their divorce made no sound.

By the Time He Got to India

Your mother took me to the movie
Around the World in Eighty Days,
Father said. It usually takes her almost that long
to forget what she was mad at me for.
But by the time the actor had gotten
to India she seemed to have forgotten
last month's incident. I don't remember
what it was. Now she's mad at me
for something else—I hadn't held her hand.
I didn't think the movie warranted
that type of attention. It wasn't
that romantic, but she said it didn't
matter what type it was—I could
hold her hand anyway & let her decide.

How to Avoid Being Idle

How to Build Confidence

I'm going to teach you how to feel confident,
Father said, in one easy lesson. Repeat
after me, "Mother is a jerk." I'm
confident she can't hear us, because
I just saw her leave the house. I'm
also confident you won't tell her what
I said, because you said it too. When
she returns I'll compliment her on her dress.
If I complimented her on anything else
she'd get suspicious. That's what
confidence is in a nutshell—knowing
what you're able to get away with.

How to Avoid Being Idle

You should always act like you're going
somewhere, Father said, even if you're not.
No one has to know you're idle.
You shouldn't be advertising it by doing nothing.
If you could avoid standing still when you're
outside that'll help people think you're doing
some form of exercise. The more you look
the part the more convincing you'll be.

Facts About Grammar

It seems rather unfair that you can
add an *s* to the word *cat* to make it
plural, Father said, but you're not allowed
to do the same to the word *fish*. Whoever
made that rule must have liked cats better.
Unless you specify the amount of fish,
there's no way of knowing if it's one
or more. Even though English
is my native tongue, I don't understand
much grammar. It seems like whoever
came up with it didn't feel that it was
his responsibility to make sure it made sense.
He left that job to someone else. I just memorize
the rules, so people won't think I'm uneducated.

The Price of Being Alone

Whatever you do is always
more enjoyable when it's done
with someone else, Father said,
unless it's a very private act,
like having to use the toilet.
But just because you read a book
alone doesn't mean you need
to be alone for everything.
When you do things by yourself
you generally keep repeating what
you have already done. But when
you're with someone the chances
of doing something different increase.

Similar Brains

I don't like to use your older sister
as an example, Father said, because
I'm afraid you might think I'm encouraging you
to imitate her bad habits.
Unfortunately, she has lots of those.
I'm only bringing her up
to remind you that she gets high grades.
Your brains must be somewhat similar,
since you both have the same parents.
The only difference is that she's using hers
at school & not at home. You're using yours
at home & not at school. I want you to use them in both places.

The Use of Facts

A bull has horns, Father said.
A cow doesn't. It's good to know
facts. You will be able to insert them
into any conversation. You
just have to make sure you
put them in the right places.
It's a little like cooking—you
have to add the ingredients
at different times, you can't
just shove them all into the pot at once.

Talking During the Commercials

It seems like the commercials are getting longer,
Father said, & the shows are getting shorter.
This is the fourth one in a row. Don't they
realize there's a limit to our patience, & we're
ready to pull the plug on the TV if they continue
to take advantage of us? I'd pull it out now
if you weren't watching it. The only reason
I'm watching it is so we can talk. The TV
gives us an excuse to be together. Otherwise,
we'd be in separate rooms. I'm sorry for
attacking the very commercials that enable
us to talk, but there's nothing else to talk about.

The Benefits of Ignorance

If ignorance is bliss, Father said,
shouldn't you be looking blissful?
You should check to see if you have
the right kind of ignorance. If you're
not getting the benefits that most people
get from acting stupid, then you should
go back to what you always were—
being too smart for your own good.

The Correct Distance
from a Crocodile

They say you should never
smile at a crocodile, Father said.
I say if you're close enough
that it can see you smiling,
then you're not where you should be.
You should be far away enough
that if it does see your face
it won't be able to make out your features.

The Benefits of an Active Lifestyle

You seem to like things the most
if you can do them while you're sitting,
Father said. It doesn't seem like it's
the books you're reading that give
you pleasure, but that you read them
while you're sitting down. You
get most of your satisfaction from doing
things that require very little physical effort.
It's not that your brain needs to be filled
with new facts, but that you have grown
accustomed to being lazy. You can learn
just as much from being active. And since
that'll put you with other active people,
none of them will have the time to sit down
& read a book to prove that the information you got was wrong.

Lengthy Services

I shouldn't applaud the rabbi while
he's delivering a sermon, Father said,
but if that embarrasses him into making
them shorter I might do it. God doesn't
need him putting words into His mouth.
If God was satisfied with the Ten Commandments
what right does the rabbi have to add on
a few more? I've been thinking of attending
another temple that has shorter services.
If it took God a second to create
the rivers, why should we have
to spend the whole night listening to the rabbi
describe how just the sight of them gives
him such spiritual bliss? He should keep
most of that information to himself & give us the short version.

What Waking Up Means

You should be grateful that I woke you up,
Father said, rather than having your alarm clock
do it. It's ineffective. You shut it off
the moment it rings. Then you go back
to sleep & don't get out of bed
until three hours later. Yet, you claim
you woke up at the time the alarm was set.
When I removed the covers from your bed
while you were still using them I was showing you
what waking up means. I know that made you
very unhappy, but you're no longer permitted
to make up your own definitions.
From now on you can only use
the ones that are in the dictionary.

Cutting Down Costs

If you only have ninety cents,
& you want to buy an item
that's priced a little higher,
Father said, what do you do?
Do you ask if you can get a discount?
Do you wait until you earn the difference?
Or do you simply not buy it?
That's the simplest solution.
What you don't get doesn't cost anything.

The Pursuit of Laziness

It seems like the only thing you learned
at college was how to be lazy, Father said.
We didn't feel the need to teach that at home.
If you had studied American history you'd
have noticed that our founding fathers
made no mention of it in the Bill of Rights.
Nowhere is it written that one has the right
to be lazy. Since you're a citizen of this country,
I'm not going to allow you to be lazy in my house.
If you don't like that rule you're free to swim
a few miles off shore where the laws
of our government don't apply. But
I doubt if you'll be able to be lazy out there.
You'd have to spend all your time just staying afloat.

What Followed Your Birth

You might not like being reminded
of your birthday, Father said,
but your mother & I do. Your
birth was a happy occasion.
What followed was both good
& bad. That was to be expected,
but what we didn't expect was
that you'd be the last of your friends
to get a job, which you still haven't
gotten yet. It just took you longer
to get started. You had to go back
to school. That wouldn't have been so bad
if you were learning something, but
after all these years to still not know
what you want for a present doesn't
speak well for education.

Undecided

Your mother & I didn't know what
to get you for a present, Father said.
We kept asking you, but you wouldn't
tell us. So we got what's good
for all occasions—a shirt. But since
we've given you that for your last three birthdays
we were hoping to give you something different.
We were thinking of just giving you cash,
but that'd have been too impersonal. Plus,
you might have saved it & not spent it.
This way even if you don't wear them we might
still get some use out of them. If you suddenly
started accusing us of never getting you anything
we could open your drawer & show you the shirts.
Just because you don't wear them doesn't negate our intent.

Abandoning the Declaration

Your sister didn't like her birthday present,
Father said, & made us return it
for a better one. She didn't deserve
the first one. When you were studying
the Declaration of Independence you
might not have noticed that children
are never mentioned. It just mentions
citizens. Only adults are that.
There, the Declaration doesn't apply
to you. Parents are free to be tyrants.
I should abandon those principles for a week,
so you can see what it was like to live
without any rights. You wouldn't
like it. That's why you should respect ours.
You shouldn't ask us to return a present
until you've unwrapped it & had a chance
to show excitement, instead of idle curiosity.

Doesn't Matter What It Looks Like

"When you have blown your nose,
you should not open your handkerchief
and inspect it, as though pearls or rubies
had dropped out of your skull."

The Book of Manners (1958)

After you have blown your nose,
Father said, it's not polite to look inside
your handkerchief to see what it looks like.
You're not a doctor. What's more important
is getting the handkerchief back into your pocket
without staining your pants. There are some things
it's better not to look at. It should be left
to your imagination, but if you have
a strong desire to look you can always
find pictures of it in a medical book.

Saving It for Later

I must be making you nervous,
Father said. Otherwise, you wouldn't
be fidgeting as much. Now what I
want to know is what have I done
that was so terrible? I can't think
of anything. I've given you nothing
to worry about. I've provided
for your basic needs. You don't
have to worry about going hungry.
You should save your nervousness
for when you really need it, like when
you get older. By that time you should
find a situation that warrants it.

No Place for It to Go

If you have a pot belly while you're
still young it'd be hard to get rid
of it when you get older, Father said.
As you get older there's a tendency
to add weight, because one becomes
less active. But if there's no room
left in your stomach for those extra
pounds, then your arms, legs & cheeks
will get fatter. Your features will
become distorted. It's important
to keep your face very much the same
or no one from the past will be able to recognize you.

Tight Bathing Suits

We went to Acapulco in Mexico
and watched these young guys
dive off cliffs, Father said. I
liked it until they got out of the water
and wanted to be compensated for the risk
they were taking. I didn't tell them
to jump or give them a push. Why
should I have to pay? So I put nothing
in their cups. One guy deliberately
shook off the water from his long hair
and got me wet. Your mother was
too busy looking at their bathing suits
to notice what was going on. When I showed her
how wet I was, she wanted to know how I could
get like that without going into the water. I pointed
to those guys and she understood. But she left with me,
so I have to commend her on her loyalty, though
I did catch her trying to sneak in one last look.

The Art of Marriage

There's an art to living together,
Father said, and since your mother
is the creative one I let her
work on it. I stand on the side
and say, "Have you finished
perfecting our marriage yet?"
"I can only accomplish that,"
she says, "by getting a new husband."
That's how I know she still loves me.
Otherwise, it wouldn't be a joke.

The Movies She Picks

I go to the movies to forget myself,
Father said. The more excitement
on the screen the easier it is to pretend
that the main character is me. Your
mother goes to find herself. The movies
she picks are so slow that the only thing
the actors know how to do is talk more.
I can't lose myself in the action if there isn't any.

No Signs of Getting Better

You went into therapy looking depressed.
Father said. After going a full year
you look even worse. Yet, your therapist
had the audacity to tell me that you've
been making great progress. At least after
you get a haircut your hair looks better,
but after seeing her you're lucky if you
look the same. The only area where
you've improved is in your cheeks.
You put on a little weight. They
look less bony. But she wasn't
the one feeding you.

Misery Loves Company

Sometimes I feel miserable,
Father said, but unlike you I don't
make a big deal of it. I just see it
as the price you pay for being human—
getting my share of the unhappiness.
Whereas, you go to a doctor to talk
about your problems, blowing them up
until they're out of proportion. I
don't blame your doctor for having
a keen eye for business—the longer
you see him the more money
he gets. I just hope he's not planning
on making you his permanent customer.

Only Your Eyes Seem to Work

I know it hurts to get something stuck in your eye,
Father said. I hated to see all those tears. But if
you look at it in a positive way you now have proof
that your eyes are doing their job. I wish I could
say the same about your other body parts. The
only time I ever see your arms move is when you're
holding a fork and are about to eat. I've never
seen you lift them higher than your mouth.

The Need to Get Away

I wouldn't want to stay home all day,
Father said, like you do. Frankly,
I don't know how you do it. I don't
plan on ever retiring. You should
make leaving the house from time to time
a habit. The key is to leave before
your mother starts yelling. If you leave
once she has already started she's
only going to use that as another thing
to yell at you about when you get back.
I'm always doing errands to get myself out
of the house. Just like a matador has
to get out of the way of a charging bull,
I have to do some fancy sidestepping
to avoid your mother. The trick is
to do it before they start thinking about charging.

Getting Me Steamed

It takes a lot to get me angry,
Father said, & even more to get me
to stay that way, but you've been
able to accomplish both feats.
I thought I told you never to start
a discussion when I'm about to fall asleep.
The fact that I was under the covers
& had my eyes closed, apparently
made no impression. If I wasn't
sleeping I was doing a close approximation
of it. What does it take to convince you?
Do you expect me to snore too?

Worth Bending Down For

If I saw a penny on the sidewalk
when I was a kid I'd push whoever
was standing closest to it out of the way,
Father said, so I could get it. Nowadays
a kid wouldn't bend down to pick up
a coin that was less than a quarter.
I know a penny isn't worth what it once was,
but it's still worth something. At times
you might feel the same way about yourself
& find yourself saying, "I'm not worth much."
But you & I came from a similar gene pool.
That fact alone should make you feel you're worth a lot.

—

Practicing for That Day

We're not going to be around forever,
Father said. One day your mother & I
are going to die. That's why it's good
we're going away for a week,
so you can practice being without us.
I know it's not the same thing. When
you die you never come back. But
by practicing for our deaths you'll
be better able to deal with them
when they do occur. It'll give you
a slight edge over the relatives.
You won't be standing around like them
wondering how it could have happened.
You'll already be somewhat used to it.
For them our deaths will be a new experience.
For you it'll be more like a memory.

Spring Cleaning Came Early

Your mother decided to do her spring cleaning
in August, Father said. She wanted to get
a head-start on the neighbors, so when
it was time to do it she could just sit back
& get pleasure from watching others work.
But the garbage men must not have appreciated
her starting that early, because they've
picked up everyone's garbarge but ours.
I hope they don't wait until spring to do it.
Just because they respect the seasons doesn't
mean everyone does. They should make
allowances for people like your mother.

Mother of Invention

They say necessity is the mother
of invention, Father said, but you
don't feel the necessity of inventing
an excuse for why you don't visit us anymore.
Your sister, who was given less than you, doesn't
visit us much either but at least she invents a new excuse
every week that she's unable to come.

The Peanut Count

I want you to eat only one salted peanut,
Father said, to test your willpower. If
you can eat only one I'll know you've
been working on it while I was at work.
But if you have to beg for more,
then we'd have to get your willpower back
to where it was before—at about five peanuts.

Reusing Words

Don't think you know everything,
Father said, just because you're good
with words. They aren't everything.
I try to say the smallest amount possible.
Instead of using them indiscriminately
I try to conserve them. I'm the only one
in this household who recycles them. I
say the same thing over & over again,
like "Who forgot to turn out the lights?
Who forgot to clean up after themselves
in the bathroom?" Since you don't listen
I never have to think of other things to say.

The Joke That Got No Laughs

You should have enough courtesy
to laugh after I tell a joke, Father said,
even if you don't find it funny.
You might find it funny later.
It's like you're giving me
your laughter in advance. You
shouldn't be asking me to tell you
where the punch line was. It's
always at the end & my joke
was no exception. I apologize if I
didn't tell it as well as I had heard it.
Or maybe it was the audience
that was at fault. You just didn't
get it. It might have been too low brow.
Maybe I should just find another family
to tell it to. I chose mine because
of the convenience. But I might have
done better if I had told it next door.

Taking Your Fun While You Can

Life is supposed to be fun
when you're a kid, Father said.
As you get to be an adult
it becomes hard work. I only
act like I'm having fun
when I'm with my family,
so your mother won't yell at me.
If you expect to wait until you
get older to have fun you might
become deeply disappointed.
When you reach my age
the only fun you'll have is remembering it.

As I Lay Dying

To Coincide

Your mother hopes we'll die at the same time,
Father said, because she won't know what
to do without me. I know she's being
romantic, but how does she expect
us to time our deaths when
she has always insisted on going first
when we walk through a door?
Finally, she wants to wait for me, so we
can die together. But I've already spent
too much time waiting for her to get ready
for things she likes. Imagine how long
she'd take getting ready for something
she dislikes. I'd rather die on my own,
so I can get the damn thing over with.

God's Delivery System

The farmers were praying for rain,
Father said, but when they got it
they weren't happy. They said
it was the wrong type. There
was too much too soon. That's
why you should be grateful
that God doesn't answer
all your prayers. You never
know how He's going to
deliver them—wholesale,
one big storm, or retail,
a nice steady drizzle.

Dressing Up for a Possible Memory

You're never certain when you're making
a memorable memory, Father said.
You only know after the fact. For instance,
take this moment. It seems no different
from thousands of others. I'm talking.
You're pretending to listen. Yet, for some
strange reason this might be the one we recall.
That's why even when I'm not working I always
dress well. If we're going to remember
this moment, I prefer that at least one of us looks good.

Taking Longer Than Your Mother

Your mother's death didn't take as long
as mine, Father said. Dying must have been
hard for her, but she made it easy for us.
Mine is hard for everyone involved,
& it still isn't over yet. I feel bad
for the work I am putting everyone through.
Each time it seems like I'm about to die
I keep thinking that I must have forgotten
to do something very important.
But when I gtt out of the coma I realize
I had already said goodbye.

Choice of Diseases

Now that I'm sick & have
all this time to contemplate
the meaning of the universe,
Father said, I understand why
I never did it before. Nothing
looks good from a prone position.
You have to walk around to appreciate
things. Once I get better I don't
intend to get sick for a while. But
if I do I hope I get one of those diseases
you can walk around with.

When the Body Breaks Down

Everyone in the hospital tries to avoid
mentioning the death word, Father said.
Meanwhile, the patients are disappearing
left & right. Not all of them could have
gone home—they wouldn't have left
their belongings behind. The nurses
& doctors can afford to treat death
like it's a game, because they're
not the ones dying. They never give
you a straight answer. "How
long," I say, "do you think it'll be
before I can walk without someone
having to hold me?" "That depends,"
they say, "on how much you want
to get better." You'd have to be be
an ignoramus to want to stay sick.
Unfortunately, just when I felt a resurgence
of brain cells, my heart got tired of working.
It was almost like I could hear it pump
less blood. It sounded like a clock
that had lost a few of its ticks.

Six-Shooter

My days are numbered, Father said.
I may never get out of this hospital alive.
I thought I had beat this disease, but
it was in remission—inside me the whole time.
When I used to watch westerns on TV
I'd dream of dying with a six-shooter
in my hand. With all the medication
I'm taking I don't think I could lift one,
or keep my arms steady enough to take aim.
Besides, I'd hate to shoot someone,
& as he lay dying he'd have to spend his last
remaining minutes wondering why he had been shot,
like I have to do with this cancer. I keep wondering
why God couldn't have given me a disease I could have beat.

A Call from Death Valley

Most people try to avoid using the word *death*
when you're talking to them from a hospital bed,
Father said. That's why when your sister called
to tell me about the wonderful time she was having
in Death Valley I had to ask her to repeat herself.
Of all of the places she could have gone to,
she picked the one with the most inappropriate name.
I had to hear her go on about the skeletons
of animals she had seen. Finally, I couldn't
stop myself from asking, "Did you see
anything that was alive?" "There were
lots of other hikers," she said. Luckily
a nurse came & I had an excuse to get off the phone.

The Trapped Sardine

The difference between dying
& surviving, Father said, is like
the difference between a sardine
in a can and one in the sea.
A dead sardine only helps
the person who eats it. But
the sardine in the sea can
make more or have more sardines,
depending on what sex it is.

Escape from the Hospital

If I was going to die I wanted to do it
at your sister's house, Father said,
so she could take care of me. When
she took me to her house after I had
signed myself out of the hospital,
I thought everything was going according
to plan until I looked out the living room window
& saw the view—one side of a hill.
I had this urge to go outside & climb
to the top, so I could see what the other
side looked like. I didn't have this problem
at the hospital, because there was nothing
to look at. Now I understand why people want to stay there.

Among Familiar Surroundings

Your mother died at your sister's house,
Father said. Unless I make a miraculous
recovery it seems like I'm going to die
here too. It's a lot more pleasant in her house
than the hospital. Dying is so common there
it may take the nurses an hour before
they even notice that you're dead
& another hour to do something about it.
You'll have plenty of time to think about
where you're going to die, but you should
seriously consider doing it here.
It'd be hard for your sister not to let you.
She wouldn't want to go against family tradition.

Saving a Spot for Me in Heaven

When I go to Heaven I'll be curious
to see who else I'll meet there, Father said,
besides your mother. She's the only one
I'm sure of meeting, since just before
she died she told me she would be saving
me a spot. I wonder how she'll handle
the fact that while she was gone I found
another girlfriend. It didn't mean anything,
but convincing her of that is going
to be very difficult, almost impossible.
I hope she already knows about it
& was able to make the proper adjustments,
or I'll just have to get away from her
by going to that other place.

One Organ Too Many

I know very little about how the body works,
Father said, but as long as it gets me to where
I want to go, I don't mind if it has to be repaired
from time to time. I can definitely think
of lots of ways it could have been designed better.
It makes me wonder what God was thinking about
when He created Adam. He must have been
exhausted from creating everything else. I wish
He could have thought of another way for me to have
kids withouth my needing a prostate gland. If I
had known I was going to get cancer there
I'd have gotten rid of it ages ago. But I couldn't
just walk into a hospital & ask for my prostate
to be removed. I first had to have a reason.
But when I finally had one it was too late.

Four Thumbs Are Better Than Two

You keep singing "This old man,
he plays one. He plays knick-knack
on his thumb," Father said. If
that old man was smarter he'd
have saved money for his old age.
He'd have been able to pay someone
to keep him occupied, so he wouldn't
have to incessantly play with his thumbs.
Or if he still preferred playing knick-knack,
he could do it with a partner—the more
thumbs there are the more fun he'd have.

Why There Are No More Miracles

God would perform miracles in the old days,
Father said, but nowadays if he set a bush
on fire, like he did for Moses, the fire department
would rush to put it out. The newspapers
would send out photographers. There'd be
an investigation. A reward would be given
to help find the arsonist. Some innocent person
would get blamed. God has enough people
believing in him. Why does He need
all that commotion for the sake of a few more?

Dying Once Is Enough

If you're in the hospital when I'm about
to die, Father said, make sure you show
the doctors the papers in which
I instructed them not to resuscitate me.
If they can make a buck by bringing me
back from the dead they'll do it gladly.
They wouldn't care what state I was in
after they were finished resuscitating.
But if you tell them your father is
only willing to die once, you'll see
how fast they stop resuscitating me.

Pushing the Future Further Ahead

It's easier to believe in God,
Father said, than not to believe in Him.
It figures you'd take the harder road.
Just promise me you won't announce
the reasons for your disbelief
while we're visiting family. It's
not the type of information relatives
need to know. They're more interested
in what you've done. And if you
haven't done much lately, like
in your case, then you should
tell them what you're planning on doing.
Don't make the future only a season away.
Make it much longer than that.
The further away you make it
the less chance there'll be
of a relative remembering
that most of it didn't come true.

All the Dead I've Known

When you've lived as long as I have,
Father said, most of the people you've
known are dead. Though, I'm still not excited
about the prospect of joining them. So if I
start feeling nauseous I just tell myself
that even though I feel very uncomfortable
I'm probably still better off here than where I'm going.
It's disappointing having to die, but it's going
to be even more so if there's no Heaven, because
no matter how difficult dying can be, death lasts longer.

The News of My Teeth

You can't get anything decent to eat
at this hospital, Father said. This
looks like baby food. I don't need
my peaches chopped up into a million pieces
that resemble mush. I have my teeth
to do that. That dietician has never
seen my teeth, or he'd have given me
something I could use them on. But
how do I go about finding him when
I'm not permitted to leave my bed? I haven't
been successful so far. Instead, I show them
to the nurses in the hope that one of them
will mention it to him & he'll correct his mistake.

God's Laugh

I'd be happy if I never saw this hospital again,
Father said. The doctors act like
they know what they're doing, but after
each operation they perform I bet God
must be laughing at them. They think they
can fix what He made not to last.
He created Adam out of dust & Eve
from Adam's rib. If He had wanted us
to live longer, He'd have used better materials.

Cemetery Plot & Stone

I'm glad I already have a cemetery plot
& stone waiting for me, Father said.
Imagine how much I'd get charged
if I tried to buy one in the condition
I'm in. The salesman would think,
"This guy will croak before he gets
the chance to compare our prices
with the competition. I'll charge
him the most that I can." But since
I got my plot & stone early, I was
able to get a good deal. Now I'm
not even sure if I got that. Will
the stone hold up or will it crack
in the middle? Should I have spent
more on a better one? The only
good thing about dying is that I
won't be around if something goes wrong.
You'll have to take care of it.

A Crooked Man

My doctor steps into my room
at the hospital, Father said, looks
at my chart, talks to me for a minute,
then leaves. The next day I get a bill
for five hundred dollars. So when
I see him again I say, "I want to get
my money's worth this time. Why
don't you stay a while." He says,
"Your insurance is paying for it.
You're not. So relax." I tell him
about the deductible. Once I spend
more than the allotted sum it comes
out of my pocket. He says I have
a ways to go. But how can I give
him my trust when I now know he's
a crook? But if I change doctors
I'll have to take all those tests again.
So I don't report him to the AMA,
but I want you to do me a favor.
After I die go over his bills very carefully.
Make sure they stop on the day of my death.

What to Save for Death

You should be thankful you're alive,
Father said. No matter how bad you're feeling
it could be a lot worse when you're dead.
No one knows what that feels like.
That's why you should take advantage
of nature—the sun on your shoulders,
the wind in your hair—because once you're dead
you may never get that opportunity again.
You may have plenty of time to indulge
in your own thoughts when you're dead.
That may be the only thing you can do..
You won't be able to walk in a meadow
if your legs don't work & your eyes stay closed.
So if I were you, I'd do more physical stuff
while you're still capable of doing it
& save the thinking for when you're dead.

Half Dead

After I get a dose of the pain medication,
Father said, I forget my problems. I feel
half dead. I want
to become even more dead. But why
should I be getting myself ready for death
when I don't want it to happen? I should
be fighting it by making plans to return
to my apartment. But when the pain
starts in again I tell myself, "You
took pride in pulling other people's legs,
getting them to believe what wasn't true.
Don't you dare do that to yourself."
When the nurse comes into the room
I accept reality. I tell her to increase the medication.

Daily Lotto

Life is this daily lottery
with death, Father said,
though if you win too soon
it's not as good a prize
as it is many years later.